pagan

Selected Poems

Kaye McDonough

New Native Press
2014

9-18-2014

for
Montre!

Thanks
so much
for coming
to Cornelia

Kaye

FIRST PRINTING

With gratitude to the usual suspects: John Geluardi, Michelle
Valladares, Elaine Sexton, Mary Lesser, Anne Taylor, Elizabeth
Hudgins (as I first knew her), George Scrivani, and Neeli Cherkovski.
To my editor and publisher, Thomas Rain Crowe, for his loyalty and
generosity, to Alan Kaufman who restored my sense of myself as a
poet and to my unfailing friend Bill Morgan.
R.I.P. Alix McQueen Geluardi.

Cover: *Winged Nike of Samothrace* from arthistoryspot.com
Part I front: Figure of *Iris* from the west pediment of the Parthenon
© British Museum at   http://www.britishmuseum.org
Part II front: *Nike Adjusting Her Sandal* from the Temple of Athena
Nike on the Acropolis, from studyblue.com

Copy Editor: Nan Watkins

Printed at: Brandt/Doubleday – Davenport, IA

New Native Press books and broadsides are published
for Thomas Rain Crowe by New Native Press. Orders
or inquiries may be addressed to: NNP, PO Box 2554,
Cullowhee, NC 28723. Email:newnativepress@hotmail.com.
website: www.newnativepress.com

ISBN: 1-883197-33-3

Library of Congress Catalog Card #: 2013952549

10 9 8 7 6 5 4 3 2 1

Contents

6

Watching Dancers to the Sufi Choir in Washington Square Park

Outtakes from the Bride of Dionysus

The Queen of Emeralds

George

I Kissed a Stone

The Stones

Dolmens and Barrows: Sex and Death the Old Way

Perseus with the Head of Medusa

The Nice People

Bribing the Muse

from *The Book of Complaints*

A Visit to the Elgin Marbles in the Dead of Winter

Gothic Conventions: Chartres Cathedral and the Rest

Rossetti's Muse

I Was Happy with Poetry

Mad Meg

A Violent End

In and Out of the Met

Parallel Realities

The Good Omen

Museum Pieces: The Vermeers

INTRODUCTION

-to Kayezee

My dear sister poet of those actually pretty wild and whacky days in San Francisco's North Beach in the '70s. How wonderful that *Pagan* has been gathered as the Selected Poems of Kaye McDonough and is being issued by Thomas Rain Crowe's New Native Press. This marks something of a circle, and I'm honored to have been asked to participate in it by writing some prefatory words to the book.

I'll put it this way: in the '70s in North Beach, Kaye and Tom and I were street poets here (I still live in North Beach) and mutual friends in the life of the coffee houses and cafes. The friendships have been enduring through the years: Tom developed into a marvelous poet and translator, as well as a publisher working out of his native North Carolina, and so it seems natural for him to want to see Kaye McDonough's poems into print.

I'll tell you why. That McDonough gal embodied the Bohemian spirit resonant to the days of Paris in the '20s perhaps more than anyone in North Beach in the '70s. And it shows up masterfully in so many of the works in this book. Of course, by the time 50 years had passed and two wars (WW2 and the Korean War) had occurred, and a third war---the American war in Vietnam---was in the process of coming to an end, the Parisian days of the so-called Lost Generation had been transformed through the Beat Generation into a world of street poets and artists. Under which umbrella Kaye McDonough sang, singing in the sun.

That's why you will read her touching and ever savvy portraits of such poets as Bob Kaufman, who, to many of us, was the political essence of the Beat Generation; Jack Micheline, a poet- painter of the innocence of the street; Robert Creeley; Robert Duncan; the renowned artist Georgia O'Keeffe; the brilliant printer and multi- lingual all-time friend of Kaye's, George Scrivani; her extraordinary portrait of Zelda Fitzgerald; and then of course her moving personal love poems to the "Frank" of her life in the 60s and Gregory Corso, who gave her what she needed most at a certain point in her life, her son Nile (now 29 and studying at Johns Hopkins), whom she brought up on the East Coast having left North Beach---in body but not in spirit---in the '80s.

Kaye had a small press in the '70s, the Greenlight Press, and published small editions of works of Micheline and Kirby Doyle, another poet on the streets of the Beach. I always have said that that spirit of Bohemia she embodied in words----and this is the important historical meaning of *Pagan*--captured the pulse of this village better than anyone in that decade. That is, if you wanted to know what was going on at the many poetry readings----sometimes three a night at different venues in an area of five streets---McDonough's poems and the drawings on napkins by Kristen Wetterhahn (thousands of them, including visitors from other countries) would reveal North Beach to you in its creative cosmopolitan essence: a village driven by the word and visual image.

But this book also has configurations of others beside dem poets and artists: I was also moved deeply by poems such as, "Vodka on Good Friday," "I Am My Own Family," "The Survivor," "Amsterdam: Six Variations," and then, as if to tiara a poetic life that saw Kayezee move from San Francisco to New England, there're the poems written on the East Coast, including the tour de force of this book, "Mad Meg," the longest and perhaps most visionary poem in the volume, and one of another voyage.

McDonough takes the forms of her poems "as they come"---that is, she allows the objects of her feelings to dictate the shapes of their expressions. And she writes always with an upwardly signaling grace, brilliance of mind, with sensitivity, humor and compassion for all who touch the keys of her resonant feelings.

You might try to, but I daresay you won't be able to turn away from this gloriously contemporary book of poems.

Jack Hirschman
San Francisco
2013

-- to my mother

to my son

pagan

Part I

A Poem for Isadora Duncan

Isadora was no jerk
In memory of her
plaster the town
with giant gestures
Picture her sailing
through the door
Pinned to her red scarf
a note that reads
'Remember Me'

   *

The pedant sips
from a crystal glass
Isadora smashes it
by way of a toast
'The room is dark,'
he complains
She lights the candle
He whimpers:
'But I am afraid to die'
'Worse yet,' says she
'afraid to live!'

*

The dancer returns to her Wild God

To a land of grapes

and vats of fire

The old Cornball, the Ham

kisses Poetry on the mouth

Isadora was no jerk!

She was Columbia driving

a white heat

The Moveable Feast

Will the Moveable Feast
kindly sit down for a minute?
I can't find you

Bob Kaufman Reading at Vesuvio's Bar

Walnut doll, wind-up man,
your arms and eyelids
are pulled by an epileptic puppeteer.
We have seen you possessed by the invisible,
mad, and mad, too, your memory streets.
Broadway blinks sad bosoms
of free women you loved.
Jazz horns, alive in your head,
hang still in pawnshop windows.
North Beach is a scavenger's museum
where the curator is Dionysus
deballed, too drunk to dream.

You taught your dance to clubfoots,
your vision to the blind.
Now you walk the streets
with matted hair and maddened feet
like a dog who's been
too long without tending.
Your dream was hit by a cab
at Broadway and Columbus.
I saw a photograph of you and Eileen
standing in a garden.

What painful apple did you eat
to hurt your eyes with such a look?
Lucifer must have turned that face to God
at his first sight of hell.

But you were born before the angels,
before the Christian god.
You were the poet before sin
and hell is not forever.

The dynamite volcano is not extinct.
We heard you at Vesuvio's singing Hart Crane.
You blew America from your mouth
and smiled your ancient vision
round a shocked barroom.
"Die, centuries, die," you sang
and two thousand years
spilled its lava in our laps.
Sodom, expecting an earthquake,
was not expecting you.

Jew not Jew,
Black not Black,
Outlaw, outcast,
an open sore in your own son's gut,

you are the poet

of lost heavens and damned gods.

Sing the dream again

that music may break

the concrete you walk

and lovers rise up from their tombs

I Have Gone Mad with Love, Love, Mad

Your stories have filled me up like a room.
I trip over your grandparents,
fall against a cousin, a wife.
Your losses hit me on the head,
hurt me with remembering.
Yesterday, I saw the boy you must have been
sitting quietly with his hands folded
at the kitchen table.
Today, I see you crossing every street
but I walk around alone, love,
looking up my feelings in bookstores,
half-drunk, beneath a half-eaten moon
that hangs across my day like a heart.

I Fell

The day's round moon
held the hill I fell down from a thread
I fell
over straw Brueghel ridges plowed with roads
I fell
over their disappearance into a shiver of blue water
where fog moved south toward Santa Cruz.

You were an Indian on the rock
looking at the Bay
recounting legends.
There were two lovers, you said.
When one was killed,
the other laid down and died.
He became Mount Diablo,
she Mount Tamalpais beneath out feet.
You tripped the catch in me.
Old times stood up in the panorama
like relatives at a reunion.
A morning of broccoli trees and artichokes
paralyzed me again with its clarity.
While you talked about Delta ghost towns
and riding the Sacramento River,

I spent the night again,
lying awake on its banks
choked with mist and childhood time.
I wanted to bring you my life on a plate.

We walked past trees of water shaking with light,
a wind of water rushing above our heads.
I fell down that hill and fell again.
You would leave poems on stones,
magic histories tied to pieces of mountain.
I fell.

When Bolinas Lagoon turned arctic blue,
you were with me
driving to find the sunset. We found
an orange oval, set in ice blue
that disappeared like a flaming lollipop
behind the Bolinas mesa.
We drove into the ice-blue refrigerator
from a yellow-wheat day
we watched from rocks
my whole life falling inside me.
We drove,
and wound back again where darkness was beginning,
cities of lights appearing through curves

and that full moon holding all our hills.
We drove and drove to home,
ate dinner,
watched television,
held each other at last,
then slept,
me before you.

I fell
down the mountain
and down the moon.
I fell.
We drove.
You were with me.

Bootleg Li Po: **On Visiting Steve Moffat**
at the Hoopa Valley Indian Reservation
and Not Finding Him at Home

Summer squashes in the garden sleep in the rain.

Dogs bark at the river turning below –

A black snake uncoils, disappears.

The sun slips away.

Piano through screen door

sits silent, unplayed.

Only two people walk the dirt road.

Neither one knows where to find my friend.

Sadly, I make a bed on the porch with the dogs.

Little Elegy for Jack Micheline (d. Feb. 27, 1998)

Street poets don't make much money,
Jack Micheline rarely had any,
lived by selling books of poems that he wrote,
lived by selling nutty watercolors he painted,
childlike portraits of men in big hats
he'd call "Ferdinand Magellan,"
or "Arthur Rimbaud."
He blew his windfalls at the track.

                    *

All morning, Jack and I drink and talk
with Armando by the bar at Vesuvio's
then leave for the Times' dollar matinee.
Blacked out in their "Ladies' Room"
from brandy Alexanders,
I miss all but beginning and end
of "The Persecution and Assassination
of Jean-Paul Marat as Performed by
the Inmates of the Asylum of Charenton
under the Direction of the Marquis de Sade,"
a movie just as long as its name.
Jack bellows, "Miss Mac-Donna,
what happened to you?"
Theatre doors open to overcast sun.

24

*

On a backstreet of the Haight,
Jack and I in my car
at the late end of evening,
poetry reading gone wrong.
Jack slams his fist on the dashboard,
punches up -- "Motherfuckers" --
breaking the windshield,
spider-webbed fragments
backlit by the moon.

*

At a jam-packed cafe,
our reading scheduled for midnight,
Howard Hart brings drums
and sax-playing friend
to the Island,
painted with palm trees.
Our poems float up
to a thin slice of moon.

*

By the side of the highway
between Phoenix and Tucson,

three a.m. night too bright for sleep,
Jack and I climb on the roof of the car,
highest, nearest place to the sky. We're dazed by
never-before-seen stars,
polluted Pittsburgh sky of my childhood
all washed clean in the light of the Pleiades.
Next day, north of Tucson,
(artists' ranch -- friends of Jack's)
broken windmill, swarms of bee-buzz,
hot butterflies hundredfold in the sun.

*

Jack died on a San Francisco BART train,
his pockets stuffed with poems, not cash,
even the month he died in short-changed.
Street poets never did make any money,
but here's what Jack Micheline left for me
the sun, the moon and stars.

Our City's Saints

Madmen and beggars roam the City of St. Francis.

One laughs to the high heavens,

no blue cat's eye

more magic

than the cocked crystal eyeball

he's set on the stars.

Another goes about in sacerdotal dress,

his kimono is a chasuble,

the blankets draped across his arm

are altar linens for a Midnight Mass

and the Eucharistic wine he's tucked beneath them:

Rasputin's Night Train Express.

Aging Tolstoy with his pack

had more to atone for

than these bhikkus.

So they pass:

        Redeemers from the Theatre

        of the Seventh Seal.

As much as St. Francis

they are the saints of our city,

the drunks, the crazies,

those god-damned bums.

Bootleg Li Po: East Coast Thoughts of Far Away San Francisco Friend

So much left behind --
Yesterday won't stay put.
Heartbroken by many confusions,
these days, sorrow follows sorrow.
From a thousand miles away, sweeping winds
whisk honking geese on Highways to Nowhere.
At the window of my house, I think about all of it
Surrealists, street poets, oracles of the Beats,
political messages, jazzy and new,
all of us cherishing free-flowing wordplay
and wild-winging thought.
Old friend, hop the ladder,
we'll climb to the sky
and swing there
from smiling corners of moon.
Steel sheets of Bay stretch coldly tonight
Sorrows come now that no wine, no drug could dull.
We know New York, even San Francisco,
are not answers to everything.
Tomorrow, I will let loose my hair
and go run by the River.

Bootleg Li Po: Songs of the Women of North Beach

San Francisco Bay waters glow

like the moon hanging

above City Lights.

Young women, tattooed,

wearing small steel rings

and studs in their ears, arrive

in the moonlight,

their faces open, agitated

as wind-driven waves.

They look somehow wounded.

Bootleg Li Po: **Saying Goodbye to a Friend**

World Trade Center Towers once cut off the view.

West of the city, Hudson River flows.

Here at Horatio Street,

we go our separate ways --

lone newspaper blowing,

hours of dark travel ahead.

Night clouds lit by headlights,

faces green in dashboard glow,

thoughts are wild horses running,

eee-oo, eee-oo, car disappears.

Vodka on Good Friday

The only reason she left Charleston, she said,
was she'd fucked every man in town worth having.
She told me her lovers numbered in the hundreds.
She'd fucked men never speaking a word,
never wanting to see them again.
She'd fucked everyone, from real estate agents
to adolescents on street corners
and she'd allowed herself love:
the weekend husband from San Jose
who filled her house with groceries and liquor.
That big woman. Twenty-six years old.
I'd have been her lover, too.
I'm loving her now with words
for all the pain that's run through her
like a human Mississippi River.
Big, sad woman.
Dark magic rose in her living room
and pain
the pain
the drunken crucifixion
drinking vodka at her house
last Good Friday afternoon
with curtains drawn on the whole world.

Discontented

Discontented
I resented
that my life
was regimented

Hypertensive
he defended
no conventions
no pretensions

I intended
to befriend him
but by passion
was prevented

I remember
in surrender
though distended
he was tender

He was splendid
me upended
I consented
Love was ended

Now I'm dead
and unlamented
killed by my love's
inattention
killed by my love's
good intentions

Independent
half demented
I revolted
then repented

Talk to Robert Creeley about It

> *"Oh well, I will say here*
> *knowing each man,*
> *let you find a good wife too,*
> *and love her as hard as you can"*
> -- Robert Creeley

I.

Breasts are your bonbons

You suck a lemon fondant

spit out a chocolate covered cherry

Vaginas you try on like finger rings

The pearl cluster is too loose perhaps

The gold band a bit too tight

You collect hearts like paintings

They are nailed to your walls

Skulls ring your house

They are the ivory necklace

fallen from the throat of your latest lady

II.

Women lie around you like mirrors
You pick up one
then another
comb your hair
adjust your features in their glass
Do you see? You grow thin
from wanting some love on your bones

The O'Keeffes

1.

The O'Keeffes
are everywhere,
subliminal and safe enough to hang
on timeshare walls,
transient
in a doctor's waiting room
cancerous
or secure behind the motel checkout desk
advertising what is "cultural,"
an art exhibit
or an opera.
Ladies in khaki skirts,
rich physicians' wives
pore over her paintings of flowers
an angry, oversized red vagina
attached to a paleolithic flaming-red butt.
Ah, they are really quite nice.
Ms O'Keeffe learned early
that if women are flowers
two coy surrealist eyes
and must only paint flowers
flirt from petunia petal faces

she'd give them what they want.
Three green eyes bed down
in purple gentians.
So be it.

Calla Lily in Tall Glass II.
One enveloping virgin-white petal
whorls around its inner phallic head.
She learned that line, expressive line is drawn slowly,
not by momentum but by force of will
compelling the whole hand, the whole arm,
not just the fingers.
Abstraction 1916
sculpted when her mother died,
rears up like a thyrsus.
She learned that resolution lies in realms of space that vibrate
in their atmospheres of dark and light
beyond real worlds of light and shade.
Jack-in-the-Pulpit, painted more than once,
Red Canna ca 1923, streaming like a fistful of red ribbons,
her famous poppies, arrogant, black at the center,
their stamens, anthers, pistils couched
in luxuriant rippling folds of red.
Take one thing, then paint it big.
Corporate.

2.

Lawrence Tree 1929.

Far from New York gallery life,

she must have lain there on her back

just beside the tree,

late at night,

gazing at what was invisible

under eastern industrial skies:

the stars

strewn helter-skelter, blazing

in fiery Blakean points --

while consumptive Lawrence

(lover of gentians and the dark)

brawled with his frowzy wife on the porch of his ranch,

the belligerent phallic thrust of the tree

directing her attention away from them, upward --

then painted what she saw,

the soaring black trunk, a rocket to the Milky Way

where form implodes

annihilating matter and the known --

then painted something else again:

clouds

indifferent to suggestive arroyos

or

a black and sovereign cross

indicting boiling crimson ground.
The landscape, New Mexico, suited me perfectly, she said.

She painted floating pelvises
free of their offspring,
they were twisted,
isolated,
flying,
then painted a skull
in High Desert,
emptied of its animal brains,
a white calico rose tucked next to the horn
where the cow's ear had been in life,
across its silenced jaws
another rose, also white,
in playful memoriam to a cud.

She painted these skulls, arroyos, crosses, flowers, clouds,
again and again.
She learned
that only paradox endures,
Pelvis with the Distance 1943
her willful line
fluid
in a sky that will not give.

Tovarich

While we are walking one evening near Caffe Trieste,
we see a friend who's known to be fond of what's Russian.
"Tovarich!" you call to him kindly.
Another man, walking in our direction, smiles and bows,
thinking the greeting has been made mistakenly to him.
"Buona sera," he says, not wanting to offend.
The four of us now come together on the corner,
smile deeply, shake hands,
make appreciative gestures to one another, then part,
a meeting of great politeness being ended.

A Calculation

Paris in the Twenties
lasted forty years

The Lost Art of Sylvia Beach

Sylvia Beach's father, a minister, performed
      marriage ceremonies for Woodrow Wilson's daughters
His own daughter ministered to writers,
      their readers, their children, their dogs
Shakespeare & Company was the Lost Generation's
      living room and Poste Restante presided over by
      a postcard rescued from Walt Whitman's wastebasket
      and a bust of the Immortal Bard
Joyce called Sylvia Beach to tend him
      when his one remaining good eye inflamed
      "Don't let them take my eye"
      She didn't
      Looked after him so well, a wag once asked her
        "How's God?"
You wouldn't want a rebuke from Sylvia Beach
Her sternest words were reserved for Robert MacAlmon
      who "neglected his craft which was supposed to be writing"
And Sylvia Beach knew when to call it quits
She dismantled Shakespeare & Company overnight
      rather than let a Nazi officer requisition
      her last copy of Finnegans Wake
He must have been surprised when he returned next day
      to find the shop completely gone, without a trace

Those adrift in the mass
in the encroaching, anonymous ugly
those hungry for the beautiful
could do worse (the poet said)
than to seek out
the lost art of Sylvia Beach

Dialogue on the Panning of Zelda Sayre Fitzgerald

> *"I liked houses under construction and often I walked on open roofs. I liked to jump from high places . . . I liked to dive and climb in the tops of trees . . . "*
>
> -- Zelda S. Fitzgerald

In the South of white rooms and young men toasting chastity
Beside the pear tree and in front of the judge she said:

> *The air shines and it is yellow and white at the same time.*
> *This is the gift air and the day holding round it*
> *I want [I wanted] to blow into life a brilliance as into a flame*
> > *to fan it*
> *I want [I wanted] you know, everything.*

She kicked away the ladder and fell down on stage

II.
> "Called on Scott Fitz and his bride
> Latter temperamental small town Southern belle. Chews gum
> – shows knees"
>
> -- A. McKaig Diaries

So she amazed Montgomery, Alabama
> (the provinces are easily amazed)
So Ring Lardner wrote her a poem
> (not one of his best efforts)
So she painted
> (grotesque, disfigured shapes . . . they did well to keep them
> in the basement)
And danced

      (awkwardly . . . appallingly second rate . . . she was just a
      vulgar exhibitionist)
And wrote
      (embarrassing.. . . . pure sentimentality . . . would never have
      had a thing published without her husband's name behind her)
So she had a child
      (and wasn't much of a mother, to hear the reports)
A husband
      (drunks, really, the two of them – but he much her better . . .
      overblown melodrama)
A lover
      (Oh , yes, the aviator . . . fancied herself a 'pioneer')
A dream
      (take a close look at that . . . romantic drivel . . . self-
      destructive narcissism if you want my opinion . . . not the
      dream of an intelligence)
So she held her own with the best of them
      (if you can call anyone from that era really first rate other than
      Edmund Wilson and he was too busy making a fool of himself
      over Edna St. Vincent Millay, another case)
And then the best of those
Well, well, so, so what?
Check Dos Passos, Rebecca West
The artists, the critics, the psychiatrists
You know, the authorities
She was mediocre and, to say the least, neurotic
Sick – and you can shut up Zelda
Shut that woman up
How could she have been who she was?
That raw girl – Stop her movement
Wasn't didn't couldn't
No. All she ever had was, let's face it, nerve

Yet she turned circles
Odd her way with it, rational Sara said
Yes, strange the way she turned
Nearly sexless, nearly oblivious
The room transfixed to check her balance
What was that dance?

III.

As if the spirit could speak only in the language
Made intelligible by death, I call to you from the ends of ruin
In words I think you'll recognize:

    While cornstalks raised silken heads to the moon
    The Montana dream slid to the edge of the plains to its ending
    The vision roped down, made to look at itself
    Not lovely, not lovely at all.
    More domestic animals and greed
    Not the singing that was wanting
    Not the song from deep in the dream
    Back to the pots and pans
    And 'Let's look at it' and 'Here it is'
    The ordinary untransformed

    You expect me to bravo this shrinking
    You expect me to sit down like a good girl
    Yodel the nap of the carpet, the teller at the bank
    Hurrah this stupor
    That the wind has been taken out of the storm
    The sorcerer exiled from his vat
    That every day, every day, nothing can happen

That sites are set on Duco Cement
and what happened in the bathroom?
Me from cartwheeling magnolia streets?
You sing about this potato you call reality
If you can, if you honestly can
And feel grateful that you aren't
You know, starving from a deadened appetite.

Zelda, Zelda, Zelda. Here, here. Now, now.
Let's do quiet her
She was just broken-hearted over something
Therapy could have fixed
Or a good man or an education
If only someone had told her
The Republic has what it's always wanted:
Official sanction that everything's OK.
What was the matter with her anyway?

If everything vast is encompassed, defined
If the life case is cracked, the mystery solved
If my line is so ordered and classified
it's robbed of all that was rare in it
If even the brutal magic of my head is institutional property
I still spit on your normal
I still spit on your ordinary
I still spit on the names you give to everything
Because I've been to the edge and fallen off
and I believe in the promise of air
Oh, what is she talking about now?
Really. She's become quite a bore, hasn't she?
Your names are excuses for failing to dream
Your names are idols to protect you from uncertainty

You who are afraid to feel, afraid to fail
Afraid to give your thoughts a shape
I call you cowards, and to my friends I say
Take heart against the wardens of perception

Well, the simple truth is she had no friends
Poor woman. Filled with self delusions
That brilliance she wanted – a total disaster
Hives and eczema are more like it
She drank too much
Got fat, got crazy
Looked ugly one day -- Hemingway said so
Had too many hangovers
Didn't have, well, you know, just didn't make it
But I did notice in the books, in the dusty books
On the dead page, there among the litany of corpses
One fact that may have been overlooked:
A real, live woman went up in flames
Midnight, March 10, 1948, wasn't it?

The Problem

Edith Sitwell loved the homosexual painter, Tchelitchew

No doubt, some psychiatrist

could have cured her of it --

'it' being, of course, her love --

but who in his right mind

calls ridding a poet of love a cure?

Methadone Clinic Blues

You go down to the methadone clinic, honey,
  then you doctor yourself with pills,
You go down to that methadone clinic, baby,
  then you swallow all those pills,
Just watchin' what you put in your body,
  is enough to make a strong man ill.

You nod out over dinner,
drop your cigarette on the floor,
You nod out over dinner, honey,
your cigarette's burning holes in the linoleum floor,
I'm sick of finding your bent spoons and cottons,
  stuffed back in the corner of that old desk drawer.

They said you'd die by thirty,
then they said by forty-four,
They said you'd be dead by thirty,
you'd never make it to forty-four,
You're sixty-seven years old – what the *hell*? –
  looks like you're gonna live for sixty-seven more.

You're a drug addict, baby,
you know you're never gonna change,
You're a diehard drug addict, baby,
  what makes me think you're gonna change?
I may as well just go ahead
and flush my life right down the drain.

So I left and moved to white bread,
out to No Man's Land,
Yes, I moved on out to white bread, baby,
it's more than I can stand,
I know it must sound crazy, honey,
but I, I miss you – you are my man.

Amsterdam -- Six Variations

1.

In the attic with my addict by the Amstel
                the wind's high
        Set your sails for the Horn!

2.

My love and I walk the embankment
        of the Amstel River
where only this morning I saw
        a mad young Dutchman launch
        a bicycle he'd mounted on pontoons --
        queer Hans Brinker
        daring the October gale
Night darks the banks of the Amstel River
        low-flying clouds fast by
        the autumn moon
Night rain pelts the Amstel River
Great galing gusts of North Sea blow!

3.

The Amstel River runs white-capped
       beneath speeding clouds
       of night-driven rain
My love and I lie safely here
       as in the cabin of a great ship
He twists his fingers like Nijinsky
       in Scheherazade
growls softly like the Russian bear
       chained in the room where
       the prankster Count
       shut in Dubrovsky
Wind gusts upon the roof -- a gale
       against set sails
I wish I had a blood-red ruby
       to set in his ear

4.

He scratches himself
     sighs
     chuckles softly
all in nodding sleep
He starts to the turning of my page

breathes upon it in sleep
Sweet is the look
        on his mad-bear face
        as he dreams
steady the sound of his breath
while wind rips at roof tiles
        backlashed by rain

Is this the wild wind Rembrandt heard
        in his autumns
        of no money?

Low we lie -- low, low in the lowlands
His breath, the wind
the dark tobacco smell of his hair

5.

Wind whips around the house
Inside I am safe -- snug --
        in a white bed in a white room
        filled with books and low light
My hand shadows the page
I am safe
Wind beats against the window,

        pounds hard upon the roof

The North Sea wind, a boatman's demon,

        gusts sails, snaps masts

Under the windswept roof I lie

        as if it were the deck of a ship

In my cabin, all wooden-walled

        and beamed in the quiet light

        I wait for sleep

A night as black as Winter's hiney

        chills this house that looks out

        on the Amstel River

Great waters run through these lowlands

Seawall, Hold!

6.

The dreaming body breathes deep peace

No wind upon a roof can bother it

The wilder the wind, the deeper the peace --

& a darting rain fly over it!

For Frank

You took all those things,
you know you did.
You broke Alix's door and Paul's door and Roger's window.
They remember you at Abe Cohn's pawnshop:

    typewriter

    radio

    one pearl necklace

    one gold ring

Then you lied about it even after I asked you.
You drank too much, too, and you weren't honest at all.
I can't remember a single good thing we ever did.
You scared the holy hell out of Dan Cassidy that night
we went hunting for methadrine.
He ran up the street while you broke holes in the wall
and threw my pocketbook out a closed window.

I knew all about death until I met you.
All the things I'd figured out you undid,
told me I was full of shit.
I had to think all over again and wonder why you and Rich
sat and cried over Fern Hill one late afternoon.
Auntie Kaye died a hard death with you, boy.

I'll bet you thought when you died I'd pretend as though
nothing ever happened.

All the rush of words and ways come running back
from past a midnight house or two.
I'm lost again thinking of you the way I used to do.
You could sit in the big brown chair again in Berkeley.
I could sit on your shoulders and hug your head
while we read the paper and listened to the rain.

Baby, baby, come back and jump on my typewriter.
I want to see the keys fly.

The Leavetaking

-- G.

Your things are everywhere,

The more I take them from the room,

the more they're there.

The sofa is filled with your habits.

I can hardly sit on it.

What a big presence you have.

Even when you're gone, you're here.

Good King Wenceslas

"Mark my footsteps, my good page
Tread thou in them boldly
Thou shalt find the winter's rage
Freeze thy blood less coldly."

These old snows

keep me company

in cold cars,

on dark streets,

in frigid rooms,

in bitter, unheatable mornings

when faucet water runs liquid ice,

when rime whitens the tan grasses

and white ice, like puffs of cloud, chokes

the asphalt pond,

its uneven surface embedded

with long, thin, wayward tracks,

as if a berserk spider spun hot glass

and laid his threads

crisscross in the night.

Some deep memory of Christmas snow

keeps me company this morning.

(I call it Christmas, not winter,

because of the holiness.)

I am in grade school.
The long, cold-emptied avenue
of sycamores many times my age,
of maples,
elms,
deleafed and twisted,
their black branches silent
against the snow-coming sky,
takes me somewhere
other than home.
Old dormered great houses,
dark as tombs against snow lawns,
watch over my progress
through spectral banks of white snow
heaped torso-high along the sidewalk,
the ice the snow
packing upon each other as I go.
My boots take hold.

Why am I walking alone here
menaced by bootprints
larger than my bootprints?
Where am I going?

I Am My Own Family

--in debt to Wayne Miller, his own ancestor

I am my own family

this head, my gentle mother, fills with night

this spine I lean on, that bears me up in water, my father

these breasts, my wife, gather sorrows like stars

and husband, my arms, carry tears

fingers are uncles and toes my aunts

grandparent knees knock griefs in the wind

and this womb is children, daughters and sons

     who I am and may never be

we, this one, gather together for thanksgivings of night

I am my own family

the arrow that never knows landing

For Frank Again

The way you're gone
you might be in another town
or somewhere near here
drinking with other friends.
You might still be you
gone to new pleasures,
I've seen it happen, too.

I am not myself any more than you are
but you'd recognize me, I think
if you knocked on my door.
My hair is longer now
parted in the middle.
I play the piano some afternoons
and sing with friends you never met.
I can bake bread.
Alix tells me I'm an artist
and will grow into an eccentric old lady
because I have a piano in my bedroom.

What would you tell me
if you stopped over?
About the darkness and the cold

or is it hot inside that box?
You've no senses left to report.
Would you tell me about long days and nights
or the poems you wrote while you were gone?
You've no memory left to hold them.

How convenient that you died.
I can make you anything I want.
You've no will to object.
You won't turn up to embarrass me
or prove me wrong.

All your humanity went with you.
Death has no frailties,
makes no mistakes.
I'm never surprised by you anymore.
Even in fantasy you do what I expect.

You are not you anymore.
You are me now
holding a pencil
pressing on paper.

The Survivor

My life happened years ago.
I am a survivor
staring at remains
fragments of shell
pieces of bone
break against each other
these pieces of death
are a hair in the page of a book
a t-shirt in an unused suitcase
yellowed scraps I hold in my hand.
Dear life
I jumped out your windows
burned out lights in my brain
fell down at night from love.
Life, it was a life I had
I read now in plant leaves
and lines of my hand.
Life, not a day goes by
I don't think of you
remember you well.

Living by a Code

-- for Bill Morgan

Remember those Thin Man movies?

They are not digitally remastered

Not available in Dolby Sound

Not so much as colorized

Plain old black and white

with Nick Charles, private eye

played by William Powell

a circumspect outsider

endorsed by petty crooks:

'Studsy Burke says you're O.K.'

No movie-star hair curls on his forehead

It's combed back straight,

his mustache trim as cat's whiskers.

He's even elegant in pajamas.

'Is he on the case?' someone asks.

His sharp wife quips, 'A case of Scotch.'

Four a.m. A young woman barges in,

hysterical, crying, waving a pistol:

'They had me in jail last night.'

Nick Charles replies,

'Don't think a thing of it.'

Dashiel Hammett

dreamed up Nick Charles

Drank like him and loved smart women.
In 1952 he went to jail on principle.
Didn't split legal hairs
Didn't take the Fifth
Never wrote a book about it
Never named one single name
Died broke.
The IRS took everything
(that's what they did
to 'pinkos' in those days)

Back in movieland,
Nick Charles lives on,
amused but watchful,
cool as a dry martini.
He slips one hand into the pocket
of his double-breasted jacket
and with the other checks to see
that, yes, his handkerchief's in place.
The basement door lurches open
leading down to darkness.
Without fault, he executes
each turn of the twisted stair.
Against impending, obfuscated shades
his white suit, impeccable, glows.

Robert Duncan's Eye

Robert Duncan's wayward eye
turned toward the sky,
his other eye, luminous, direct,
turned to the world

When he was a boy, the poet said,
he ran across the snow to his mother,
across the snow
the snow
to the embrace of his mother
his eye cut through by sunglass shards
The snow held too much light

We know this by his eye

Museum Pieces: **St Francis by Bellini**
-- The Frick

One plain note

in an ocean of furs,

rock in the midst

of velvet.

A skull, sandals,

an ass, a crane,

St. Francis

renouncing

filigreed skies.

Museum Pieces: **The Horse Fair by Rosa Bonheur**
                    -- Metropolitan Museum

All the feel of

an afternoon

dappled on

the rear end

of a horse

Museum Pieces: **Two Turners**
       -- The Frick

In the midst of these portraits

the Turners set sail

Museum Pieces: **The Fortune Teller by Georges de La Tour**
-- Metropolitan Museum

A beautiful young woman
black-haired, black-eyed
watches her cohort snip
a watch chain inscribed:

    Fides Amor

It belongs to her victim
a well-dressed, arrogant youth
engrossed in the soothsaying
of an old fortune teller
He is oblivious to the sly fingers
that dip into his stylish pocket
Youth, Beauty, Wealth, Good Fortune

      Nothing lasts.

A Rothko Retrospective

1.

In the early work,

lips, an arm severed at the elbow,

one eye

float Osiris-like

through empty space in a well-defined field.

No Isis.

2.

A roomful of seaside,

a roomful of doors

thrown open to July beaches,

each panel lit from within by white sun.

On the floor above,

large objects pushed into place

for another installation

rumble like thunder.

A New York, a Venice,

glows through the brush strokes

of a darkening rectangular sea.

3.

More paintings like doors,
some opened, most closed,
one set on fire:
a rectangle pulsing
black as the black hole
inside clenched eyes,
a black stain on the mind's interior radiance,
a black brand forced into a field of fire.
On another canvas,
a red rectangle
won't stay put,
pulsing red as sunlit blood.

4.

No more beach, no more city.
Three panels like windows
on a starless, weatherless night,
three grey window shades drawn against it,
three flat windows that look upon
nothing but night.

5.

Silhouettes of gallery visitors
come,

then go,

across the fields of black on black

like mourners not knowing

which way to turn,

toward or away from

the inconsolable blocks.

At the Window

If I were somewhere quiet
Just with God and me
The Deaths, the Woes, all left behind,
Life's cruel Anxieties

I'd think upon the wheeling Stars
The burning Stars so bright,
I'd put my head out the window
In a deep, cool box of Night.

*

I wish I were somewhere quiet
Just with God and me.
No god, you say, all right then,
Say 'Eternity"

I'd think upon the wheeling Stars
The burning Stars so bright
Put my head out the window
In a deep, cool box of Night

The Open Question

They said my Uncle died.
When I looked upon his body
so recently vacated
I saw it was a husk,
familiar in form but empty
of all that he was.

His remains were laid to rest
like a June bug's shell
in a kid's treasure chest.

Now a childish question
stays with me
unshakable as Eternity.
Though his casket lid
is shut and bolted,
is my Uncle dead
or has he simply moulted?

In a New York Minute

The shadow across the sun
I saw reflected in a pool
is eternal eclipse
the full moon
above a New York rooftop
eternal light

The eyes that looked on them
are forever my eyes
each pair, each time, my eyes
and what they saw, me, now

On that hotel corner
twelve years ago
I was drunk among strangers
lost in a taxicab
In that moment I
will never know where I was
and midnight is irrevocable

Bootleg Li Po: **The Long Road**

A good bottle of wine costs ten bucks a pop,

Those raviolis from the Village?

Five fifty a box!

I don't care about any of it --

I'm sick of rich food and booze makes me crazy.

I get out my car keys

and turn in every direction.

I'd go north to Vermont, but the cold weather's coming,

I'd drive south to New York, but the traffic's too heavy,

I'd sit with my son at Sleeping Giant by the stream,

but suddenly I dream of rafting Brown's Canyon,

or climbing Mount Tamalpais in the rain.

The journey is long,

The journey is long,

with many directions.

How do I know which one to follow?

Someday, I will fly away on a great gust of wind,

up and over the broad and churning ocean,

on my way to some Paris in the Twenties,

across the deep and redtide seas.

Bootleg Li Po: **Thinking Back to Golden Gate Park in the Sixties**

-- to George Scrivani

Where beaded free spirits danced beneath eucalyptus trees
wrecked souls drag cardboard boxes for homes.
Nobody will even give them a quarter.
The worst burger and fries costs three bucks a pop,
Can't even get a cheap drunk anymore.

Weasels and sharks
pretend to be great men.
Hyenas guard the gate.
The roads turn in every direction.
Which one to take?
The one to high mountains
is blocked off in fog.
Our old Masters dance there
with Li Po and Blake,
where sky circles sky
and the Immortal Bay
        gleams below.

The Sixties ended long ago,
a dream within a dream.

When we were together

in San Francisco in the old days,

brandy flowed,

the jukebox played Billie Holiday songs without end.

We drained the cup

and never dreamed

darkness would follow darkness.

Old friend,

your hair thins,

mine streaks with grey.

I have fallen among Confucians

dressed in Taoist clothing.

Nobody has time to play anymore.

Our brilliant world

turns violent and cruel.

Tomorrow, I will phone you again

and we'll talk away the sorrows of the coming thousand years.

Thoughts Aboard a German Train

The hot dog border police
checked the train
I hate to call that ominous
yet it was all coming:
the numbness
& the great drifts of snow
As the nets lower over us
we even thank them

I Am Moving with Blinders

I am moving with blinders
through a field of water
I cannot identify species
my blind faith I hope is sure
or I will surely drown
in this night of water
uncertain as a porpoise in the Ganges
blinded by spiritual ablutions
they tell me I pass manta rays
they tell me I taste salt
so these are fish
so this is water

Afternoon

I sit going mad on a chair
A fly measures the hallway

Road to Chaco Canyon

Fifteen miles down washboard dirt road,
aroma of pinyon piled in the back seat,
night coming fast, dirt road disappearing,
three horses trot freely from nowhere, from brush.
Bareback and black, across broken-down bridge,
they stop in the car's path,
their eyes without fear, jet black in the twilight,
their eyes without fear, gaze on desert grasslands --
once dark, deep and hidden by seas --
where Paleo-Indians hunted in Pleistocene
Jet frog, jet black, inlaid in turquoise,
containers of turquoise, the hematite bird,
effigy pottery, human head vessel,
Cibola whiteware, striped Chuska-black bowl,
copper bell, deer bone, painted stone mortar,
black and white beads of shell and of stone,
three pieces of turquoise hid in a wall niche.
Town of Wijiji constructed at Chaco,
concentric curves of three walls of kiva,
Pueblo Bonito metates and manos,
sandstone courses of walls of Kin Kletso,
West Mesa, South Mesa, Casa Rinconada,
Mockingbird Canyon, Atlatl Cave,

Pueblo del Arroyo, Penasco Blanco,
Chimney Rock, Crownpoint, Chetro Ketl cliffs.
Rust-red shadows slip down the mesas
entering darkness of steep-sided channels.
Three horses run off, no riders, no reins.

Bootleg Li Po: Roads in Taos

Sangre de Cristos -- vast, dark --

heady with mist,

Blue Lake's heart wounded.

At night here, dirt roads

lead out to the mesa.

On cliffs of great gorge,

lone sorrows stand still.

Night owl hurries home,

but I can't find my way back.

Don't want the road

where one motel follows another.

Black Corn

-for Vijay

Among the worn-out, old white couples

who this October evening fill the lobby

of the La Fonda Hotel in Santa Fe

lopes a lone young male,

Indian or Hispanic -- maybe both, I can't tell --

tall in his cowboy boots, cowboy shirt and jeans,

as healthy as a horse,

his long and shining hair as fine

as the silk of black corn, if corn were black.

Twenty-five tops, he must be less than half my age.

To think that in my lifetime two people

made this young man out of nothing

but themselves. What beauty!

created not by scientists, not by artists,

but by lovers (aren't parents lovers?).

Who were they, in their prime, and what

did they look like, I wonder --

like gods? Or were they just

ordinary people taken by the moment?

The young man smiles,

not a movie star smile,

but a real smile,

at a real someone,

showing his well-formed teeth that are as white
as the immaculate whites of his eyes.
He flicks his head in her direction
and his black hair moves
like the silk of black corn,
if there were black corn
streaming black cornsilk.

Encounters in Taos

-- in memory of

At Leo's adobe in high mesa country,
blue Taos Mountain is framed in our window.
Slate skies backdrop chamisa and sheep.
Thunderclap on thunderclap. The adobe house darkens.
White shocks thunderbolt, thundercrack across the sky,
unloosing punishing tantrums of rain
that pour down the Great Gorge, flash flooding arroyos.

Night rain comes down, black at our window,
I open the back door to hear waters running,
forcing their way through our neighbor's acequias.
High wind gusts in and bangs our screen door.

Leo's gone down to Santa Fe. I sit at the kitchen table
late into the night, listening to the wind, the banging door
and the rain. Well past midnight, tiny brown things
whirl in like a mini-squall. What are they?
Not leaves. They're alive. Not bugs,
but a host of small frogs, confused by the storm.
Another night, a cold one, I sat on the doorstep
and cried for a long time. The next morning,
stretched across it, a large, black snake.

All this happened summers and summers ago
in Taos, when I lived there with Leo,
who has, since then, married and divorced.

The Sin

Pregnant I feel like a walking aquarium,
the creature inside me flipping
       like some marvelous fish!
One day he'll beach to strange new shores
       where catty predators wait
       with nets of morality.

This coming nativity my mother sees as Doomsday.
"But you're not married! Pity the poor child!
       Think of the neighbors!"
She wails tearily into the phone Bible stories
       of the Woman at the Well
while I long to set sail like Noah in his Ark.

The man who made this life in me
       knows it is holy,
creation sinless as a midnight sea.
As for me, I know I have cast my bread
       wide upon the waters.
Let only the fishes of the sea
       bear witness against me.

For His Eleventh Birthday, My Son
Rides Horseback in Canyon de Chelly

My son as he was
on a blanket-backed horse,
my son as he was
with the reins,
my son as he was
with the reins in his hand
on a blanket-backed horse
in a river of sand.
A blanket-backed horse
in a canyon of sand,
petroglyph messages
scratched in the stone,
my son as he was with the reins.
On a blanket-backed horse
with a Navajo boy,
my son as he rode
with the reins in his hand
on haunches of horse
through pools of quicksand,
zigzags and mazes
cut in the rock
of Canyon de Chelly

with the rain falling down,
my son, my son, my son,
my son as he was with the reins,
rode into the Canyon,
cantering, cantering.

Watching Dancers to the Sufi Choir
in Washington Square Park

I bring my dark humors
to light in the park.
Young women, young children
turn heads in a ring
The dance they spin
from sunstruck hairs
screws my open, empty places
to the birth of night.
I rotate, a blackening spiral

Young women, dance with your children
in every green park
draw filaments of light from the day
haloes to hold what must be let go
There are no units to measure this flow
no name to give this loss I feel
only rings you make
that bind my darkness like heat

Part II

Outtakes from the Bride of Dionysus

The Bride of Dionysus retired to her colonial house in Connecticut
with a kitchen as trim and as white as a nurse.
When the door slammed shut, the photos closed their eyes.
Books cracked on their shelves.
Snow fell.
That summer, the grass was cut within an inch of its life.

> *Everything's been taken care of*
> *Almost everything's been taken care of*
> *Everything's been taken care of*
> *except the Bride of Dionysus.*

The Bride of Dionysus failed to live up to expectations.
The Bride of Dionysus would not go the limit.
The Bride of Dionysus proved to be unstable.
The Bride of Dionysus was unfit for servitude.
The Bride of Dionysus was independently wealthy.
She resigned -- took it all with her.
She wears a disguise now.
No one can find her.
The Bride of Dionysus is no longer the Bride of Dionysus.

The Queen of Emeralds

I was the patron saint
of the Sorcerer's Apprentice.
When he conjured me,
I dropped from my head
twelve stars that took the shape
of a Celtic cross in the southern sky.
A cerulean blue scarf flew out my sleeve.
He wrapped it around his waist
and ended up on the Bering Straits.

Following his departure,
I kissed a stone.
It fractured to forty
perfectly faceted emeralds.
For this, they named me
Queen of Emeralds,
but I was trying to make
the stone speak.

George

--for George again

George in earrings,
speaking Greek,
high hat and flip,
as arrogant as a prince.

George, the Marquis,
the Count in ruby rings
whose eyes turn topaz,
whose black hair lies
against his face
like onyx rings
on an alabaster plate.

George, the Head of the Monastery,
Moralist, Scribe,
suffering from
a complete state of grace,
shoots rainbows,
plaits snakes,
counts the angels
that genderlessly twirl
upon the heads
of astounded pins.

Headstrong,

cocksure,

right,

he pitches down flights

of dizzy stars.

     *

When George is in a passion,

young men change to women,

women to men.

Titania caresses Oberon,

faery inventors spirit the wood.

If George feels sorrow,

tree leaves go limp,

wildflowers sigh against the rocks

and all the enchantments of Prospero

lie discarded in the sand.

Should George leave,

what shades he'd loose,

what killing gloom!

No heated music

would play from caves,

no warm-eyed badger
waddle from the bush,
and this dumb world would wheel
among deserted stars.

In death, George will roll back
the azure scroll of the sky
and by his wand will guide
departed souls to realms of Hades,
not to Hell, against which
he has cast his charms.

All fears will fall away
as he recounts his tales:
the one about Leander
who swam the Hellespont by night,
the one about Orpheus
whose lyre moved the stones.

I Kissed a Stone

I kissed a stone
To make it speak
It said: *What* are you doing?

The Stones

You were older than me.
I was older than them.
The stones lurked
in the background,
worn smooth
by lifetimes of weather

*

I was surprised to see the stones!
I mean, they were so old.
Naturally, all stones are old
(What else would they be?)
but these looked it.
They were solid rock, all right.

The stones were so
The stones were so
The stones were so old!

Dolmens and Barrows: Sex and Death the Old Way

At the airport in Pittsburgh, en route to my cousin
for the final goodbye --he's dying of brain tumors --
a respectful person should think weighty thoughts about death.
But just like my barbarian ancestor Celts,
my (hopefully) un-tumored, uncivilized brain
finds relief in archeological porn.
As parents, aunts, uncles, cousins, old lovers
drop dead around me, I now understand
the ancient tribes knew what they were doing.
All across Britain, right at the sites of gravestones and barrows,
they paid homage to their great male phallus,
raising monuments to Neolithic sex, Pictish sex,
Roman sex, Celtic sex, Norman sex,
a northerly counterpoint to the be-boobed
Cycladic mamas of the Mediterranean.

Maybe some long-ago ancestor of mine helped build
the burial chamber at Trethevy Quoit -- I'd like to think so --
          where a huge phallic rock floats atop heads of seven others.
Like giant erections, countless such rocks were raised -- I'm all for
          them:
the horn-shaped forecourt of the stones of Cairnholy,
the great Stripple Stones that stud Hawks Tor Downs.

Out in the open, like hollies, like scrub oaks,
nothing furtive about them,
they belong to the landscape,
survive blasted weather,
arrows of rock everywhere, as different as lovers:
the Glamis stone etched with a fine Celtic cross
surrounded by centaur and four-legged beast.
Its opposite side bears Pictish inscriptions
of mirror, of fish, of life-giving snake.
Runes run in bands on Bewcastle Cross.
Double spirals of female and male circle dogs, circle hawks.
Like entwined lovers, knots interlock on its face,
sex and death forever interlaced.

On the outermost isles of the Hebrides,
oysters, cast up from the wild, open sea,
litter the shores with their ungathered pearls.
A promontory juts to the lap of Loch Roag
where thirteen stones of Callanish Circle
dwarf twin cairns enclosed in their breadth.
They plunge deep in their beds. They crush the wild thyme.
Below the horizon wait quicksilver springs.
Night's eye, night's breath, heathers the barrows.
A standing stone enters the moon.

Perseus with the Head of Medusa

The statue of Perseus,
holding the severed Head of Medusa,
is set like a jewel in the balustrade
that crowns the central staircase
of the Metropolitan Museum of Art.

New York's slick hero smiles
contentedly to himself
that he has sliced the head
from this woman's body.
Medusa's face records
the horror of his act.

O the cut Perseus had to make
to claim himself this victory.
It wasn't her look
that changed his world to stone.

The Nice People

The nice people
ground out
everybody else.

Bribing the Muse

What should I do?
The muse is a woman like me.

Must I forever regard her
in the mirror of a man's eye
or must I the Lady in the Tower be,
some form of muse myself?

What am I going to do
when my eyes are two quick and radiant matches,
when small weights heavier than lust
drop inside my wrists?
O Muse! I must have you!

With looks more wild than Christabel's
I'll charm the count for you,
seduce Dionysus, throwing round you
his fabulous skin.

Let the world around us
lie indifferent as a coin!
I'll come to you like Pushkin
with lace at my throat,

at the candlelit ball waltz you
all the way to Armageddon,
ride you away in a troika
through the moon-frosted snow
beneath sinister black branches
of waiting trees.
Nothing will harm you.
Your perfect beauty is safe with me.

Here, I've brought you a present:
my heart on a plate.
Eat it. We shall never die.

Dark and heavy the blood stains my windowsill.
Its red heat burns holes in the snow.

from *The Book of Complaints*

-- for the Winged Wondrous Wainio

Too much quaffing & wanness

Too many wouldst thous & wilts

I mean, where are we anyway?

If you can't talk American

go back to the castle

Whaddya think this is around here, bub?

Arcady or what?

Pack up your dried roses

Strap them to the giraffe

& wend thou thy way.

A Visit to the Elgin Marbles in the Dead of Winter

1.

Doorways close on other doorways.

Listen at an ancient stair.

Lightless corridors greet lightless courts.

Labyrinths of muffled sound,

Celtic, Saxon, suggest some distress.

As for me, I carry a small torch

strictly for black passage to a closed church

and travertine gate. By this glow I pass

a midnight channel, haunted by snow,

ringed in stones carved in cipher.

Iced ponds, fountains frozen at the mouth

are sure signs of the season.

The monstrous portal swings wide its gates.

Within, a room seduces me -- Courage, Take heart.

2.

Zeus, whose brain had ached with her,

(Athena, within, the child of his ruptured thought,

waiting to break the bondage of his understanding)

splits open in masculine birth, all head,

divulging fullblown, magnificent Pallas Athene.
There's the invisible, plundered center.

Voluptuous figures languor in satisfaction
that she is equal to her task.
Saved! against onslaughts of steel,
against onslaughts of glass, the marbles
are saved by her perfect strength.

Blizzard fields and glaciers birthed
in the deadest recess of time
cringe before a greater cold. The gibberish
of amazement at last is translated.
Dumbfounded pilgrims come to worship
at the foot of undulating stone.

Gothic Conventions: Chartres Cathedral and the Rest

1.

I notice in the Life of the Virgin
the godchild is worshipped on a pedestal
while the mother dreams in a box
The kings and queens stand by
still waiting for the Last Judgement
But stone can make only so many demands
And a hell of a lot of somebodies
Raised some mighty asymmetrical steeples
They dwarf even Christ of the Apocalypse
and that entombed woman

2.

There's patient Pythagoras
tooling over another theorem
squat and longsuffering
trying to make reason in a recess of a church

If you have to be stone
(and sooner or later it does come to that)
better to be the Klaus Sluter mourner
at the tomb of Philip the Bold –
he appears to be holding his nose –

or better yet that open air gargoyle
the one with the horns and the wings
atop a bell tower at the Cathedral of Notre Dame
He leans on his elbows overlooking Paris
with his head in his hands and his tongue stuck out

I think: Ah, yes. When it comes to stone
I know what's best
But something still bothers me
about that woman in the box

Rossetti's Muse

Rossetti buried poems with his wife & model, Elizabeth Siddal [Beata Beatrix], dead from an overdose of laudanum. Later he thought better of it and had her exhumed so that he could retrieve them.

The great Muse is silent, unmoving beauty
on which the Creator meditates,
the divinity of her inert, unneedy calm
the locus for his flights & storms.

What did they see in Jane Morris
with her strange hairline
oversized lips & that colossal nose?
Perhaps the soar of her swanlike neck --
More likely her heavy-lidded somnolence.

Rossetti quaffs his opiates.
The mute Sphinx stares
nothing of pain, nothing of passion
in the slow infinity of her look.
She dreams the Lethe realms
where odalisques recline
& ruined landscapes long accustomed
to their wrecks rest darkly in forgotten decline.

The great swan's neck of Jane,

her dark, drugged gaze preside.

Rossetti loses himself in dream,

sets the vision in oils,

then goes home to frolic with his wombat.

He knew to wrest his poems from the grave.

Long, long had they lain in Morphia's tresses

Golden, golden were they, even in death.

I Was Happy with Poetry

I was happy with Poetry
It sang me Swan Songs
late at night
It flashed its eyes
and cared about everything

I will love it til
the day of my death
when it will take me
in its great arms

I'm sorry to leave you
nothing but dust.

Mad Meg

--to Kristen, Tisa, Anne, Elizabeth, Mary, Elaine, Michelle,
and to my dearest poetry friend Alix McQueen Geluardi

PART I

She assembled a crew in a time of a great confusion:
       Aphrodite was repulsive,
       Pallas Athene had become hopelessly stupid,
       even Demeter had renounced corn.
So, she took Grace of the even temper & furious eyes,
       Anne, of the long body & long limb,
       Nancy of clever stitches,
She took Ellen who broke thimbles,
       Ruth of the fractured plate,
She took the Gentlewoman Kate
       who laced harpsichords & repaired skates, SHE
She chose Sandra of the maddening laugh   ASSEMBLES
       & Zinta, a displaced Greek,   A CREW
She took the dancer, Patricia,
       & she who loved to paint,
She took Iseult, the sad-eyed,
       & the daredevil, Jane,
She took the wildhaired poet
       who lived by the riverbed
       & she, the poet of the Little Creek,
She took Sara of the Kilted Skirt
       & Alona of thistledown,
She gathered the strong jaw, the melting eye
       & Lynn of the nervous gesture,
She took the horsewoman,

Kristen, the healer,
    & she who rescued skulls,
She took the roper of ponies
    & Alice the Sage
She took Deborah of the big knuckle & brutal grip,
    Judith of the Javelins
    & Victoria, the lover of adolescent boys.

She called to the Maiden of the Bound Feet
    whose wrist had been imprisoned
    by an oval of jade.
"Crack the jade!" & purposefully did it break.   THE NATURE
    Color slowed in the unmending pieces   OF JADE
    turning a mood of anger to milk.
She called to Circe, tired of pigs,
    to Medea, fatigued by blood.
Then she beckoned Penelope
    & Penelope was truly sick of the loom.
At the last, she took Edith, the builder of arches,
    a nike, a maenad, a mourner,
    Doris of the Crowbar,
    four attempted suicides, three drunks,
    two lunatics and a speed freak.
She left behind the kissass, the turncoat
    & the zipped lip.
Round her neck a necklace bare
    the teeth of sycophants, dipshits & simps,
    strands of hair from those
    who let the moment pass.
She stood on deck, stared deep in the eye of each
    & gave a reason:
    "I love you"

"Speak to me"
   "Call my name"

At that time each person lived apart
   in a misunderstanding of shadows,
   lost tribes, echoes in the forest,   THE
   a memory of skin.   TIMES
They wanted a history & a place
   "O for a lyric!"
   "O for a song!" she cried
but the story was forgotten
& the song a distracted geography.

A terrible anger rose in her for the love of things
   "In the Name of The Mother, The Daughter,
   & The Holy Alive Being!"
She would seek the Land of the Robot King
   to rob him of the skin he possessed,
   a lynx, of magic properties.
She stomped her foot & sailed forward
   into a formidable midnight.

The ship spun through the night of water rising.   THEY
Continents rose up & glistened in the moonlight   SET SAIL
   & all the star-impacted, legend-spangled
   night did wrap these sailors round.

She called Elizabeth who knew the secret
   of unravelling water.
   "Decipher the sky" she said
& Elizabeth was joined by the poet of the Little Creek
   who sang a song of midnight.

When the song ended, a witch
      whose warts had fallen off recounted
      the Tale of Creation:
      "In the beginning, God created herself
          in her own image.
    She made forty universes,
          dumped trees & kodachrome skies.
    She admired her wheeling nests of light,   A
    then, in the third hour of the fourth day   RUDIMENTARY
    in a fit of pique, on one boomeranging planet CREATION
    she made a woman

         & in her bounty & playfulness, a man,
         for she was a god who loved to see
         what would happen.
    The woman spoke in tongues
         & loved the man's body.
    His hair fell off, regrew.
    His skin turned white.
    He aged, he was young.
    For this he cried:
         'Your god is weak
         Expunge her name!'
    & weak was a way of saying what she was.
    She fell through the remains of Europe.
    It was a sad falling & all her legends
         were torn from her."
With these words, the Tale ended.

Ashore, the thousand walls pounded to dust
      & not a soot this brown of powdered brick,   THE DUST

a cloud of dust arose & more than cloud STORM
it was an atmosphere of swirling pieces FOLLOWED BY
     of earth & wall & particles of stone, LIGHTNING
     fine, ground down to silt,
     the down of stone,
     unfiltered air dense with sedimentine snow.
Then a lightning freaked across the sky,
     a wrack!
The water jolted, envolted,
     zigzag shocks ablaze new eve
          "Stone wall! Rain pour down!
          An avalanche of midnight!"

She desired night & a horror,
the time had been too sweet
     & that clean.
The ship became a train
     moving backwards through a black hole.
The present receded.
The stars were replaced by indirect lighting.
They knew speed & the sensation of travelling.
     Fingernails grew dirty,
     brickblack buildings flipped by
     & a rude conductor clipped THE TRAIN RIDE
     diamonds in their tickets.
The nausea began, the fever
     & a clammy heat preceding vomit.
A universal sickness was upon them
     from the backward rocking motion.
Their vomit was golden & army green,
     laced with red webs.
All manner of half-digested things

issued from them
& they were glad to be purged
& begin again.
A lead-grey sky backdropped buildings
   with their eyes punched out
   "One Hundred & Twenty-Fifth Street!"   125th STREET
   Grafted smiles,
   backyards piled with discarded tires
   were emblems of an age.
They wanted to pass through it
   but were beset by razors.
They were plagued by smalltime hoods.
A white frame house went mad with grief.
She was anonymous
   & taught them to ride Gorky subways
   late at night.
Trains roared by, screeched, ungreased
   "All right, All right!" she cried
      "Blow hair!"

She longed for pretense & self-deception,
   the soft-focus of platitudes.
She blabbed on as if her words had
   great significance.
Sycophancy & degradation, mediocrity,   THE CONDITION
   the loss of personal honor   IN NEED OF
   were bywords of this time.   REDEMPTION
She recognized what she had become
   & felt disgust.
She looked within & moved herself away
   from convenience.
That was a start,

    & with steel wool & cornstarch
    began the loosing of the leeches
    that were intimate with her blood.
This took longer than she had expected
    & she missed the suckers.
She herself was a true parasite,
    though she found this difficult to face.
She felt superior to who she was.
She sang of this and her song was a long one
    & frequently boring,
    but the crew listened
    as there was little else to do.

Dark brown was the color then:
    mudflats, streaked windows.
She loved low-lying diners
    & rotting piers
    & there, running down
    the black hill, a rill.
O dark time, lit by ugly lights!   SURVIVAL
    Rain, stained walls,   IN SLAG
    wired skies, slag.
She whistled & felt a love
    for ruin & rank.
She wanted to run her tongue along
    furred teeth
    & press her cheek against
    a many-sweated chest.
Windows made her sick with distance.
Streetlights stuck in her throat.
She fell in love with sleaze
    & craved bourbon breath.

The sleaze, enticing sleaze,
     replete with many marvels.
She called to life a longing for love.

They sailed on through cliffs of ice.
Snow starched their faces.   THE ICE
Breaths raised frosted flower wreaths in the air,   CLIFFS
     white lace, crystalline moons in various phases:
     the quarter freeze, the half cold, the iced full.
Their song at that time was snow
     "Wasted snow" they sang "Wasted, wasted snow!"

Suddenly, the water made a shield
     & bore them boatways
     & then exclaimed at a joke not too funny.
     The crew tilted.
She had burst the bubble.
"You're ruining it!" one cried.
     "Oh, no" was her reply
     "I embellish!"
     & she who laughed too loudly   THE JOKE
     laughed with her.
Together they dispelled the moment.
Their rising laughter took the air
     & wound patterns of exquisite
     faery's hair.
It traced pinioned heels,
     shed dazzled down.
     "Tricky waters where we go!"
She laughed her laugh
     "Send me a hard news, a brittle day!
     I do not blanch!" she cried.

PART II

They found the Land of the Robot King,
        but the lynx skin was lost
        & all the kingdom lay in rusty desolation.   THE LAND
They used a phone that stole dimes,   OF THE
an adding machine that couldn't count,   ROBOT
        stopped escalators, steaming air conditioners, KING
        a typewriter missing three vowels.
Images flopped on screens.
Fuses blew.
She turned off the TV
        & disconnected the halogen lamp.
She pushed a car over a cliff.
By the cliff, at the foot of a tree,
        she found a dead bird, coated in oil.   THE
She gauzed & nested it in a shoebox   REDEMPTION
        & buried it one foot deep in the ground.
All this to restore an era of grace.
She murdered the wife
        & for this she was called a hater of men,
        but this was either a lie
        or a misunderstanding because
she took a man by his hand,
        dived in his eye,
        walked around inside his hair
        & lived another epic that was totally his.
She kissed his feet.
She kissed his teeth.
She marvelled his spine
        & set herself around his love.
She married his eyes

& levelled them with
the letting go of his wishes.
She kissed his lids closed & he slept.

"What was wanted was something beautiful:
a song,
the throat of a living bird!"
She was interested in those warm-blooded,
beating creatures of divided hearts
& mammals forgotten in aluminum forests,
so she made an invocation:
"O Musk Ox, Mule Deer, Ground Squirrel, Moose,
O Ptarmigan & Black Bear,   THE
Grey Fox, White Sheep, Mountain Goat,   INVOCATION
Opossum, Porcupine & Hare,   TO LIFE
Antelope, Coyote, Cacomistle, Skunk,
Caribou & Beaver gnawing at the trunk
of poplar, alder, pine, live oak"
She diverted into trees & went on:
"Red Maple, Canoe Birch,
Quaking Aspen, O, all the trees
& bushes of Azalea, Mariposa, Juniper,
O tufts of Sedge & Bunchberries."
Here, she looked to the top of a tree
"By the Sky!" she exclaimed
& lapsed into a coma of birds:
"Woodpecker, PeeWee, O Snowy Owl with feathered feet,
Goldfinch, Catbird, Chimneyswift,
Kite & Falcon, Boobie, Tern,
Cuckoo, Kiwi, Emu, Quail!
They fly, they fly, these Hoopoes, these Shrikes
& Bitterns, Bustards, Rails & Coots!"

The crew feared that she had become delirious.
    "Scarlet Tanager, Barnswallow, I sing you!
    Housewren, you Waxwing, you Red-Tailed Hawk!"
A derangement had disordered her features.
Her eyes turned black.
A tenderness softened the amassing lines of defense.
    "Let the bitter language shatter on the sidewalk!
    Let the hard words hurl themselves against walls!
    O delicious faces!" she acknowledged her crew
    "Let me touch you!" and she skid into a dream.

She dreamed a dream which when spoken
    did not follow text.
She dreamed a season of winter,
    compressed to frigid night.   HER DREAM:
She felt a hemorrhage & feared death.   THE
A color ran from her, not the color they name MISCARRIAGE
    'blood red,' but blood real,
the blood she carried that spun blood webs
    round shaping soul fell from her
    like molten snow.
She loosed the life & bore the scar,
    as a mollusk that's moved will leave a mark.
"What are you saying?" "Should you say this?"
In answer, she cried "Yes, O Yes!"
    "My blood is brilliant!"
    & she felt a warm hand smooth
    the unsettled hairs from her forehead.

Three pelicans dived to the east
    & one other, small, collapsed his wings
    to fall a frightening drop.

The bird struck the water, furious,
  went in needle clean,
  his protected feathers dry at the nub.
The bird did dive & went in water
  to thread his beak with fish.
All along the shipside swam a school
  of shining fishes there,
  a move they made of shimmering below
the water they were in did break & backcomb,   NIGHT OF
  foaming white followed by a calm, green,   THE
  bathtub-like fluorescence.   FLYING
The school beneath travelled in a shining mass,   FISHES:
  aswim & amove they passed there,   TRANSCENDENCE
  as stars astound a night.
Winging there with fins, they did rise to water level,
  & broke the film of difference that held them in the water.
From green in night the shining-sided fishes
  moved to water level
  & did evacuate to air,
above the water, fishes gilled the air,
  the air above the water, becoming sky-fishes flying.
There at masthead now the flaming-sided fishes flew.
They rose up in the night sky & high they breathed the air.

O gentle sky of Southern Cross,
no wind disturbed,
  save movement made by fish whose flying
  barely shook the sails.
The fish sailed & snaked the southern sky
  & rose & rose to studded black,
the vapor points of stars & fishes mingling
  set off night's flares of crimson-banded light

& citron stars, the rainbow-sided fishes flying!
They took this as a good omen
    & named it the Night of the Flying Fishes
    or, the Transcendence of the Water.
The inverted environment was reassuring to them.

In the morning, the sun struck shore
    & nasturtiums, that one on board had
    called 'ugly weed,' blazed orange
    & spat yellow tongues.
The flowers riddled cliffs & roots ran wild.
She loved them & gathered some dandelions there,
    lion-maned grass, the rampant
    fork-leaved weeds she plucked.
Milky sap stuck their hands.
They gathered clovers' hive-shaped blooms
    of white & lavender-indented feet
    & made rings of imperilled fireflies that night.
Surely tortured were these poor flying things
    but the muted rings they made
    were more beautiful than any neon.   THE ISLE
The crew wore chains of daisies   OF JOY
    & in all the common grass they played,
    day there was as gentle as night.
The Goddess of the Sun & the Goddess of the Moon
    held back the Wind
    & allowed them a rest there
    in the happiest of heats.
They threw off ropes & made an understanding
    that Praise was more difficult to mouth
    than Woe.
They talked infrequently & sniffed the sun.

130

The memory stayed deep in the flesh
    & loosed the locked joints of the time.
They were moved by light & made it a memory.

PART III

One's back had broken.
One had dived across the bow.
One who engaged the raptures of the deep
    had sailed from shipboard to deep death.   ENDING
One died frozen in smiles.
One had cut her hand.
Another merely lost a shoe.
In the course of the voyage, many things
    had happened to all of them.
She remembered their names
    & read their souls
    & had to admit she'd made many errors.
Still she stayed in the mood of plunge
    & directed the ship onward
    in her self-righteous ignorance.
She was close to a hope & to an extravagance.
She had wanted companions
    & they had enjoyed her follies.

She drew the ship to their homeland now,
    where white houses hilled the last ground
    before the setting sun.
Pigeons, grey & brown, flew up
    & gulls, egret, pelicans.
Tales of the Voyage had gone before her.

Those who waited for her named her:
      Mad Meg, Queen of Hags,
but we knew her differently.
We called her Margaret,
      she who loved to sail.

A Violent End

When he shook her
diamonds & horseshoes fell out.
Then she turned into an arch.

In and Out of the Met

-- to Chris Felver

1.

Archeological Finds

Looking into the newly-renovated Greek Galleries,

I notice five young art students, all women,

making charcoal studies of the "Venus Genetrix,"

each young woman, like each drawing, provocative,

as near to real-life Aphrodites

as this Roman copy is to its Greek original,

a bronze by Kallimachos.

A label reads that the statue,

'sleeveless in her ungirt chiton,'

lifts one edge of her 'himation' (a cloak)

with her right hand. The other, now missing,

probably held an apple.

2.

Couples

Leaving the Greek Galleries,

by chance I run into a photographer

I knew long ago in San Francisco,

with him his friend,

a woman older than he is.

We settle into the museum café
for a long afternoon's chat,
near us a couple in matching
pink vinyl minisuits
with standup pink collars that encircle
their shaved heads the way pastel paper strips cradle
kids' dyed Easter eggs.
Dining tête-à-tête,
they look happy.
My friend says he's seen them 'everywhere.'
They turn up in Paris, for example,
or in Venice for the Biennale.
They're German, he tells me,
as if to explain them,
performance artists of a sort.

3.

The Mime
Late in the day in front of the Met as I leave,
a street artist wrapped in a winding cloth,
bulletproof within his swaths of veil,
his make-up-whitened face a mask,
stands motionless,
centered on one of the fountains there

looking so much a part of it
that he might have been
commissioned as a statue.

I recognize his costume and his pose:
the Veiled Dancer, a classical Greek bronze,
thought to represent the dancer mimes
for which ancient Alexandria was famous,
peddled in replica at the gift shop.

His eyes case the crowd.
The timing's right.
He makes his moves.
He pulls,
he strains
inside the winding sheet as if
it strangled him,
he twists,
he swings his hips about and then
with studied female grace,
a magician at his self-created circus,
he abracadabras the cloth,
Salome-like,
as graceful as Odette-Odile,
working it like taffy.

A young woman presses
a coin into his hand.
He palms it
and makes it disappear.
Beside him, she looks
prosaic in her jeans.
The patsies, like me,
just can't help themselves.
We smile and toss
our dollar bills his way.

Stepping from his pedestal
he sheds his drapery skin
unveiling Nikes, a T-shirt
and pants that bag.
His dais -- a bucket --
doubles as his portmanteau
in which he stashes
whiteface and his sheet.
Quick as a hitman, he spits
in the fountain,
then leaves, taking
ancient Alexandria hostage.

4.

Apparition

Strolling down Fifth Avenue
along the stone promenade,
I put up my umbrella against
the rain. By now it's dark.
Central Park views blink
through tree trunks.
I stop to watch the miniature pools the rain makes
wink across the surface of a small lake.
Along the path of the lake's curving contour,
slowed by their spiked heels,
smiling like androgynous geishas
beneath pink umbrellas
that shield their bald heads from the rain,
comes the ubiquitous German couple,
as diminutive in the distance
as Chinese Immortals
painted on a temple screen.
They advance through the landscape,
panel by panel,
step by measured step.

Parallel Realities

Cool October, early a.m., losing myself
in what I think is Greenwich Village -- possibly Soho --
I come upon a cafe misnamed "Twelve Chairs."
In fact, it has thirty. Deep and narrow,
exposed to the street by one window, one door
it looks like a painting of a European cafe.
Inside, a mirror hung on one exposed-brick wall
reflects figures of real passersby --
a man in a hat inspecting a parking meter,
a woman rushing past carrying a briefcase --
creating the illusion of an animated painting
that I can study as I drink my coffee.
A small photographic exhibit on another wall
includes a portrait of an African-American man,
his head only, shown in three-quarter view,
his single photographed eye, watchful.
A real African-American man,
full-size, wearing an overcoat,
sits on one of the thirty chairs
talking with his friend who sits on another.
They are painters, not picture painters,
as you might expect, but house painters.
He has a fear, he tells his friend,

of falling from his catwalk.

I eat my eggs while jotting down

a thought or two:

Life is a dream.

This poem is not a pipe.

The Good Omen

Late morning,
swift white clouds
in serious motion against blue skies
scattershoot light
through Bleecker Street trees.
Leaf shadows descend
as sudden as a waterfall
down the closed backdoors
of an unmarked truck
flooring it
through an arc of foliage.
I turn away,
down Thompson to Prince.
One blown down feather, electrified,
sticks to the window
of the Kokopelli jewelry shop.
It slides around the corner of the pane,
then, like a talisman, drifts
into the recessed doorway of the store.

Museum Pieces: **The Vermeers**

-- Metropolitan Museum

He painted women
trapped in rooms,
but he furnished them
with windows and a map.

Here, he's given
one a lover,
one a lute
and all a light
about each torso plays.

Acknowlegements

Poems in *Pagan* have appeared in the following anthologies
and little magazines:

City Lights Anthology 1974
Ends and Beginnings: City Lights Review #66 1994
Exquisite Corpse 1985
The Stiffest of the Corpse: An Exquisite Corpse Reader, City Lights 1989
Outlaw Bible of American Poetry, Thunder's Mouth Press 1999
Café Society: Photographs and Poetry from San Francisco's North Beach 1978
185, Mongrel Press 1973
The Baby Beats & The 2ⁿᵈ San Francisco Renaissance:
        (bilingual French English), La Main Courante 2005
Beatitude: issues #21 1975; #23 1976; *#24* 1976; #29 1979;
        20ᵗʰ Anniversary Issue 1981; #31 1981; #32 1982;
        33 Silver 1985; #34 1987; *Beatitude Golden* 2009.
Patria Letteratura: Rivista internazionale di lingua & letteratura
        transl. Alessandra Bava (Rome, Italy, May 2013).
New College Review 2007-08
Umbra #5 Latin/Soul 1974
Long Shot: Gregory Corso Remembered 2001
Ragged Lion: A Tribute to Jack Micheline 1999
Would You Wear My Eyes? A Tribute to Bob Kaufman 1989
Chimera, Baby Beats Number #5, England 2006
Amerus: An International Journal 1979
The Holy Earth MegaScene #1 1982
The Punctual Actual Weekly, 1976
This Is (Ahem) #2 of *Black Draught Journal* 1976
Pickpocket Poems & Art and broadside, Sore Dove Press 2006
7 Carmine 2001, 2002, 2003, 2004
Lovelights 1972, 1973, 1976

Global City Review: It's All Relative, #19, CUNY 2008
5 AM Issue #13 2000
Phoenix 1973
BARD #6 1991
Poetry SF: Winter Solstice Issue #3 1985
Cenizas #16 1982
19 + 1: An Anthology of San Francisco Poetry, Second Coming Press 1978

144

Author Autobiography

Born in Pittsburgh, Pennsylvania, in 1943 (a good time to be born), raised in the fifties (a dreamlike time to be raised), lived in Berkeley in the sixties (a strange time to have survived). There I first met living, breathing poets. Spent the next twenty years in pre-gentrified San Francisco among poets, artists and friends in search of the Moveable Feast, doing readings, working with Alix Geluardi on her *185* and on my own Greenlight Press. *Zelda: Frontier Life in America* was published by City Lights in 1978. Legal troubles with the Fitzgerald estate followed. Became involved with Gregory Corso, poet master of prestidigitation and legerdemain, who stood the ancient world on its head. We lived together for a time and had a son, Nile Corso, in 1984. Moved back East in the wake of family illnesses to raise Nile, now 29 studying at Johns Hopkins. I work as an adjunct lecturer at various colleges and universities in the New Haven area and am currently working on a memoir: *The Spell of Bohemia.*

I often think back to a pilgrimage my friend Elizabeth and I made to Europe when we were just nineteen and heard the Acropolis speak.